STUDY IN THE NETHERLANDS:
Unlocking Academic Excellence in the Lowlands

Your Complete Guide to Thriving in Dutch Universities and Embracing Cultural Enrichment Abroad

Brandy Roberts

Copyright © 2024 Brandy Roberts

All rights reserved

CONTENTS

Chapter 1: Introduction...6
    Overview of the Dutch Education System................ 6
    Advantages of Pursuing Education in the Netherlands... 7
    Distinctive Characteristics of Dutch Universities and Colleges...10

Chapter 2: Choosing the Right Program and Institution... 14
    Different Types of Institutions in the Netherlands... 14
    Popular Fields of Study and Programs in the Netherlands.. 20
    Factors to Consider When Choosing a Program and Institution... 27

Chapter 3: Application Process and Admission Requirements...33
    Step-by-Step Guide to the Application Process for International Students... 33
    Admission Requirements for International Students... 41
    Tips for Crafting an Effective Personal Statement or Motivation Letter... 46
    Sample Personal Statement for a Master's Program in Environmental Science.. 52
    Sample Motivation Letter for a Bachelor's Program in International Business... 54

Chapter 4: Financing Your Studies in the Netherlands.. 58
    Comprehensive Summary of Tuition Fees for International Students in the Netherlands...............59

Financial Support Options for International Students. 63

Living Expenses and Effective Budgeting for Students in the Netherlands................................... 70

Chapter 5: Living in the Netherlands....................... 77

Accommodation Choices in the Netherlands.......... 77

Getting around: Public transportation, cycling culture, and exploring Dutch cities......................... 84

Adapting to Dutch Culture and Integrating into Society... 90

Chapter 6: Academic Life and Campus Culture...... 96

Academic calendar and grading system in the Netherlands... 96

Classroom dynamics and teaching styles............. 102

Extracurricular activities, student organizations, and social life on campus.. 108

Chapter 7: Language and Cultural Challenges...... 114

Language barriers and resources for learning Dutch. 114

Understanding Dutch customs, etiquette, and cultural norms... 120

Overcoming cultural differences and building cross-cultural competence................................... 124

Chapter 8: Employment and Career Opportunities..... 130

Regulations for International Students' Work Permits 130

Internship opportunities and gaining practical experience during your studies............................ 136

Post-graduation options: Job search strategies, entrepreneurship, and staying in the Netherlands

after graduation..142
Chapter 9: Health and Well-being........................... 148
   Healthcare System in the Netherlands and Health Insurance Obligations for Students.......................148
   Enhancing Mental Health Support Services and Resources...153
   Maintaining a Balanced Lifestyle during Studies.. 158
Chapter 10: Conclusion and Next Steps................. 163
Appendices.. 168
   Glossary of Dutch Terms Related to Education and Student Life:...168
   Directory of Useful Websites, Organizations, and Contact Information.. 173

Chapter 1: Introduction

Overview of the Dutch Education System

The Dutch educational framework is internationally esteemed for its quality, ingenuity, and inclusiveness. It comprises primary and secondary education, vocational training, and higher education. At the tertiary level, there are primarily two types of institutions: research universities and universities of applied sciences. Research universities emphasize theoretical knowledge and scientific research, while universities of applied sciences offer more hands-on, practical programs tailored to specific professions. Alongside these, private institutions provide specialized education in various domains.

Advantages of Pursuing Education in the Netherlands

Studying in the Netherlands holds several benefits for international students, making it a popular choice for higher education. These advantages include:

Academic Excellence: Dutch universities consistently rank among the world's best, renowned for their exceptional academic offerings, research opportunities, and expert faculty.

English-Language Programs: The Netherlands stands out for its extensive selection of programs taught entirely in English, appealing to non-Dutch-speaking international students.

Diverse Learning Environment: With students from over 160 nationalities, Dutch universities foster a multicultural atmosphere, enriching the educational experience and preparing students for global citizenship.

Innovative Teaching Approaches: Dutch institutions prioritize interactive, student-centric learning methods that cultivate critical thinking, collaboration, and problem-solving skills.

Affordability: Compared to other study destinations, Dutch tuition fees are relatively affordable, supplemented by numerous scholarship and financial aid opportunities.

Career Prospects: The Netherlands' thriving economy presents ample internship, job, and research prospects across various sectors, including technology, business, and innovation.

Distinctive Characteristics of Dutch Universities and Colleges

Dutch higher education institutions possess several distinguishing features:

- Interdisciplinary Focus: Many Dutch universities promote interdisciplinary learning, allowing students to explore diverse fields and tailor their education to their interests.

- Research Emphasis: Research is integral to Dutch higher education, providing students with opportunities to engage in cutting-edge projects and collaborate with faculty members.

- Modern Facilities: Equipped with state-of-the-art resources, including laboratories and libraries, Dutch universities offer students access to cutting-edge facilities and technology.

- Comprehensive Support Services: Institutions prioritize student well-being, offering academic guidance, career counseling, mental health support, and extracurricular activities.

- Commitment to Sustainability: Many Dutch universities emphasize sustainability and social responsibility, integrating these principles into their academic programs and campus initiatives.

In essence, studying in the Netherlands promises a distinctive educational journey marked by academic rigor, cultural diversity, and innovative learning opportunities. Whether pursuing traditional disciplines or exploring emerging fields, students can anticipate being intellectually stimulated and prepared to make meaningful contributions to society.

Chapter 2: Choosing the Right Program and Institution

Different Types of Institutions in the Netherlands

- **Research Universities:**

Dutch research universities are renowned for their emphasis on academic research and theoretical education. They offer a variety of undergraduate, graduate, and doctoral programs across different fields. These universities prioritize critical thinking, analytical skills, and research-driven learning.

Faculty members at research universities are often leading experts in their fields, conducting groundbreaking research and contributing to global scholarly discussions. Students benefit from engaging in research projects, collaborating with faculty mentors, and participating in academic events.

Some of the prominent research universities in the Netherlands include the University of Amsterdam, Leiden University, Utrecht University, and Wageningen University & Research. These institutions offer diverse programs in humanities, social sciences, natural sciences, engineering, and medicine, attracting students worldwide seeking rigorous academic training.

- **Universities of Applied Sciences (Hogescholen):**

Universities of Applied Sciences, or hogescholen, provide practical, hands-on education tailored to specific professions. These institutions focus on preparing students for the workforce through internships, work placements, and industry collaborations. They emphasize skills development and experiential learning.

Students at universities of applied sciences gain industry insights, technical expertise, and professional competencies relevant to their careers. These institutions prioritize collaboration with employers, offering opportunities for students to engage with industry partners and build professional networks.

Examples of universities of applied sciences in the Netherlands include Rotterdam University of Applied Sciences, Hanze University of Applied Sciences Groningen, Fontys University of Applied Sciences, and HAN University of Applied Sciences. **They offer** programs in business, engineering, hospitality, arts, media, and healthcare.

- **Private Institutions:**

Private institutions in the Netherlands offer specialized programs catering to specific industries or niche markets. They vary in size, reputation, and focus, offering innovative teaching methods and unique program offerings. Private institutions are flexible and responsive to market demand, adapting quickly to emerging trends.

These institutions may offer smaller class sizes, personalized attention, and a strong sense of community. Examples include

Nyenrode Business University, Webster University Leiden, Wittenborg University of Applied Sciences, and Hotelschool The Hague, attracting students seeking specialized education and international exposure.

In summary, the Netherlands offers diverse educational opportunities across research universities, universities of applied sciences, and private institutions. Students can find institutions aligning with their interests and career goals, whether pursuing theoretical research, vocational training, or specialized education.

Popular Fields of Study and Programs in the Netherlands

- Engineering and Technology:

The Netherlands is globally recognized for its excellence in engineering and technology, making it a favored choice for students seeking education in these domains. Disciplines like civil engineering, mechanical engineering, electrical engineering, and computer science attract students keen on acquiring advanced knowledge and research opportunities.

Leading institutions such as Delft University of Technology (TU Delft) and Eindhoven University of Technology (TU/e) **stand out for** their comprehensive programs integrating theoretical understanding with practical applications. These programs equip students with the necessary skills to tackle intricate challenges in sustainable infrastructure, renewable energy, and advanced manufacturing.

- Business and Management:

Business education remains immensely popular among international students, drawn to the Netherlands for its quality education and global career prospects. Renowned business schools offering programs in international business, finance, marketing, entrepreneurship, and management are highly sought after.

Institutions like Rotterdam School of Management (RSM), Amsterdam Business School (ABS), and Nyenrode Business University are esteemed for their rigorous curriculum, hands-on learning experiences, and strong ties to the corporate world. These programs prepare students to navigate the complexities of global business environments and emerge as leaders in their fields.

- Social Sciences and Humanities:

The Netherlands boasts a vibrant academic landscape in social sciences and humanities, attracting students intrigued by human behavior, societal dynamics, cultural nuances, and historical contexts. Programs spanning psychology, sociology, political science, anthropology, history, and cultural studies offer interdisciplinary perspectives on pressing social issues.

Institutions such as the University of Amsterdam (UvA), Leiden University, and Utrecht University excel in delivering social sciences and humanities education, offering diverse programs taught by renowned scholars and researchers. These programs foster critical thinking, intellectual curiosity, and engagement with contemporary societal and cultural dialogues, preparing students for impactful contributions to society.

- Health Sciences:

With a strong emphasis on healthcare innovation and research, health sciences programs entice students aspiring to careers in medicine, biomedical sciences, nursing, public health, and healthcare management. The Netherlands hosts world-class medical schools, research hubs, and teaching hospitals providing comprehensive education and training in healthcare disciplines. Institutions like Erasmus University Rotterdam (EUR), University Medical Center Groningen (UMCG), and Maastricht University are recognized for their state-of-the-art research infrastructure, multidisciplinary educational approach, and focus on patient-centric care. These programs equip students with the expertise, skills, and clinical exposure necessary to excel in diverse healthcare settings and contribute to global health advancement.

In summary, the Netherlands offers a plethora of popular fields of study and programs tailored to the interests, ambitions, and professional aspirations of international students. Whether pursuing education in engineering, business, social sciences, humanities, or health sciences, students can anticipate receiving top-tier education, acquiring valuable skills, and embarking on fulfilling academic and professional endeavors.

Factors to Consider When Choosing a Program and Institution

1. Academic Standing:

The reputation of both the institution and program is crucial. Research their academic standing, rankings, and accreditation to ensure quality and recognition. Look into faculty expertise, research output, and alumni achievements to gauge academic excellence.

2. Curriculum:

Review the program's curriculum to ensure it matches your academic interests, career objectives, and preferred learning style. Evaluate course offerings, specialization options, and practical components like internships or research projects. Consider how flexible the curriculum is and if it allows for interdisciplinary study.

3. Accreditation:

Check if the institution and program are accredited by relevant bodies. Accreditation confirms that the program meets set standards of quality, bolstering the credibility of your degree. Verify accreditation with respected organizations and regulatory bodies to ensure your education meets recognized standards.

4. Location:

Consider factors such as geographical setting, proximity to cities or industry centers, climate, culture, and lifestyle preferences. Assess transportation options and opportunities for cultural immersion and recreation.

5. Cost and Financial Aid:

Evaluate tuition fees, living expenses, and available financial aid options such as scholarships, grants, loans, and work-study programs. Compare costs across different programs and institutions, factoring in currency exchange rates and living expenses.

6. Language Requirements:

Determine the language of instruction and ensure you meet proficiency requirements. Consider language support services and opportunities for language improvement.

7. Career Support:

Explore internship and job placement services offered by the institution. Assess industry connections, alumni networks, and the institution's track record in placing graduates in relevant positions.

8. Student Services:

Evaluate the availability and quality of student support services, including academic advising, counseling, tutoring, and disability services. Consider the institution's commitment to student success and well-being.

9. Campus Culture:

Assess campus culture, diversity, and inclusivity. Look into opportunities for cultural exchange, intercultural dialogue, and participation in clubs and organizations.

10. Alumni Network:

Research the institution's alumni network and reputation within your chosen industry. Consider alumni success stories and the institution's alumni engagement initiatives.

By considering these factors thoughtfully, you can make a well-informed decision when choosing the right program and institution for your higher education journey.

Chapter 3: Application Process and Admission Requirements

Step-by-Step Guide to the Application Process for International Students

1. Explore Institutions and Programs:

Begin by researching universities and programs that match your academic interests and career goals. For instance, if you're keen on environmental science, explore offerings at Wageningen University & Research.

Dive into their websites, attend virtual or physical information sessions, and connect with admissions officers for further insights.

2. Collect Necessary Documents:

Understand the application requirements for each program you're eyeing and compile a checklist of required documents.

Gather items like academic transcripts, standardized test scores (e.g., TOEFL or IELTS), recommendation letters, and a personal statement.

For example, if aiming for a master's in business administration at Rotterdam School of Management (RSM), gather your undergraduate transcripts, TOEFL/IELTS scores, recommendations, and personal statement.

3. Take Language Proficiency Tests:

If mandated by institutions, prepare for and take language proficiency exams such as TOEFL or IELTS.

Plan and schedule your test in advance, allowing ample time for preparation.

Suppose your program requires a TOEFL score of 100; ensure you aim for that score and plan your test accordingly.

4. Arrange Academic Transcripts:

Request official transcripts from your prior educational institutions.

If transcripts are in a language other than English, arrange for translation and notarization.

For instance, if your undergrad was in China, request official transcripts and translate them into English if needed.

5. Craft Personal Statement or Motivation Letter:

Write a compelling personal statement or motivation letter spotlighting your academic achievements, career aspirations, and reasons for selecting the program and institution.

Tailor each statement to reflect your genuine interest and fit.

For instance, if applying to Wageningen University & Research for environmental science, discuss your sustainability passion and relevant experiences.

6. Secure Letters of Recommendation: Approach professors, employers, or mentors for strong recommendation letters.

Provide them with relevant details about your achievements, goals, and targeted programs.

For example, request a recommendation from a professor who can vouch for your academic prowess and research potential.

7. Submit Application Materials:

Complete online application forms for each chosen institution and program.

Upload or mail all required documents, including transcripts, test scores, recommendations, and personal statements.

Pay application fees and meet submission deadlines.

If applying to various Dutch programs, ensure to complete each application and submit documents before deadlines.

8. Follow Up:

After submission, check in with institutions to confirm receipt of all materials.

Maintain organization and track communication with admissions offices.

For example, send a follow-up email to ensure transcripts arrived and inquire about any additional requirements.

9. Prepare for Additional Requirements:

Some programs may necessitate interviews, tests, or portfolio submissions.

Prepare accordingly by researching common interview questions and gathering necessary materials.

If applying to a design program requiring a portfolio, ensure yours is ready to showcase your skills.

10.   Await Admission Decisions:

Once applications are submitted, patiently await admission decisions.

Monitor emails and application portals for updates on your status.

If an admission decision is delayed, follow up with the institution.

For instance, regularly check your email for notifications or log in to application portals for decision updates.

By adhering to these steps and strategies, you can effectively navigate the application process as an international student, increasing your chances of gaining admission to desired programs and institutions in the Netherlands.

Admission Requirements for International Students

- Language Proficiency Tests:

Many Dutch universities mandate that international students demonstrate proficiency in English since most programs are conducted in this language.

Commonly accepted language proficiency exams include the IELTS (International English Language Testing System) and the TOEFL (Test of English as a Foreign Language).

The IELTS evaluates English skills across four areas: listening, reading, writing, and speaking, with scores ranging from 1 to 9. Similarly, the TOEFL assesses English proficiency through reading, listening, speaking, and writing sections, yielding scores from 0 to 120.

Each university establishes its own minimum score requirements for these exams, so it's vital to verify the specifics for each institution and program of interest.

- Academic Qualifications:

Apart from language proficiency, Dutch universities have academic standards that applicants must meet.

For undergraduate programs, international students generally need equivalent qualifications to the Dutch pre-university education (VWO) diploma.

Graduate program applicants typically require a bachelor's degree or equivalent from a recognized institution.

Some programs may stipulate specific prerequisite courses or minimum GPA criteria, necessitating careful review of academic qualifications for each program.

Additionally, certain programs might demand relevant work experience or subject-specific background knowledge, particularly in specialized fields for graduate studies.

Suppose you're an international student interested in pursuing a master's in Environmental Science at Utrecht University in the Netherlands.

Utrecht University mandates international applicants to exhibit English proficiency by achieving a minimum IELTS score of 6.5 (with no subsection below 6.0) or a TOEFL iBT score of at least 93.

Additionally, applicants should hold a bachelor's degree or its equivalent from an accredited institution, preferably in a pertinent field like environmental science or biology.

Moreover, candidates may need to furnish a CV, recommendation letters, and a statement of purpose delineating their academic background, research interests, and program motivations.

By grasping these admission prerequisites, you can ensure alignment with the necessary qualifications and compile a robust application for Utrecht University's Environmental Science program.

Tips for Crafting an Effective Personal Statement or Motivation Letter

- Authenticity Matters:

Be genuine and sincere in your writing, sharing personal experiences and insights that reflect your true passions and aspirations.

Avoid clichés and instead focus on unique anecdotes and perspectives that showcase your individuality.

Example: Rather than stating a generic passion for environmental sustainability, express how your upbringing in a coastal town sparked your dedication to preserving marine ecosystems.

- Highlight Achievements and Experiences:

Emphasize academic accomplishments, extracurricular activities, volunteer work, internships, and other relevant experiences that demonstrate your readiness for the program.

Provide specific examples and stories to illustrate your skills, achievements, and contributions.

Example: Instead of a general claim about leadership abilities, offer a specific instance, such as leading a successful beach clean-up campaign as president of the Environmental Club.

- Demonstrate Fit with the Program:

Customize your statement for each institution, showing your understanding of their values, goals, and strengths.

Explain why the program aligns with your academic and career objectives.

Example: Discuss specific program features or faculty expertise that attract you, such as the Sustainable Development track at Tilburg University, and how it complements your aspirations.

- Articulate Future Plans and Goals:

Clearly outline your long-term career ambitions and how the program will contribute to their realization.

Showcase ambition and vision, demonstrating that you have a clear trajectory for your future.

Example: Instead of a vague desire to impact public health, articulate a concrete goal, such as establishing a non-profit to address healthcare disparities, and how the program at Maastricht University supports this vision.

- Maintain Consciousness and Structure: Keep your statement concise, typically within 500-800 words, and ensure a clear and organized structure.

Start with a compelling introduction, delve into different aspects of your background and motivations in the body paragraphs, and conclude with a strong summary.

Example: Craft an engaging opening sentence, use paragraphs to explore various facets of your journey, and end with a powerful conclusion that reinforces your enthusiasm.

- Revise and Proofread:

Thoroughly review your statement for grammatical errors, typos, and overall coherence.

Seek feedback from mentors or peers to refine your writing and ensure clarity and impact.

Example: Take breaks between drafts to revise with fresh perspective, and utilize feedback to enhance the statement's effectiveness before submission.

By implementing these strategies and adapting examples to your own experiences, you can create a compelling personal statement or motivation letter that effectively communicates your qualifications and aspirations to admissions committees.

Sample Personal Statement for a Master's Program in Environmental Science

Growing up in a coastal town, I cultivated a profound connection with nature, igniting a lifelong commitment to environmental conservation. Throughout my undergraduate studies in Biology, I actively pursued opportunities to delve into environmental research and initiatives. For instance, I spearheaded a project examining the impact of microplastics on marine life, gaining invaluable insights into ecosystem dynamics. My involvement in the Environmental Club further strengthened my leadership skills and passion for advocacy through organizing beach clean-ups and educational workshops. Seeking admission to the Master's program in Environmental Science at [University Name], I am excited about the program's interdisciplinary approach and emphasis on sustainability. The opportunity to collaborate with esteemed faculty and engage in cutting-edge research aligns perfectly with my academic and career goals. I aspire to leverage this program to make tangible contributions to environmental stewardship and foster a more sustainable future.

Sample Motivation Letter for a Bachelor's Program in International Business

Dear Admissions Committee,

I am eager to express my keen interest in the Bachelor's program in International Business at [University Name]. With a multicultural background and a passion for global commerce, I am enthusiastic about the opportunity to immerse myself in a rigorous academic environment that fosters cross-cultural understanding and prepares students for success in the international arena.

Having lived in diverse countries, I possess a deep appreciation for cultural diversity and a nuanced understanding of global markets. Through participation in Model United Nations conferences and entrepreneurship competitions, I honed my communication skills and strategic thinking, preparing me for the challenges of the global business landscape.

The comprehensive curriculum offered by [University Name], coupled with its emphasis on experiential learning and industry partnerships, resonates strongly with my academic and professional aspirations. I am particularly drawn to the prospect of gaining practical insights through internships and studying alongside peers from diverse backgrounds.

In summary, I am confident that the Bachelor's program in International Business at [University Name] will equip me with the knowledge, skills, and connections necessary to thrive in the global marketplace. I am eager to contribute to the university's vibrant academic community and am committed to pursuing excellence in both my studies and future career endeavors.

Thank you for considering my application. I look forward to the opportunity to contribute to the dynamic learning environment at [University Name].

Sincerely,
[Your Name]

Chapter 4: Financing Your Studies in the Netherlands

Studying abroad can be a rewarding experience, but it often comes with financial considerations. In this chapter, various aspects of financing your studies in the Netherlands will be explored, including tuition fees, scholarships, grants, financial aid opportunities, cost of living, and budgeting tips.

Comprehensive Summary of Tuition Fees for International Students in the Netherlands

The Netherlands is renowned for its top-notch education system, attracting students from around the globe. Yet, grasping the intricacies of tuition fees for international students is pivotal for prospective candidates.

Here's a condensed overview:

1. Bachelor's Programs:

Bachelor's program fees vary based on institution type and specific curriculum.

On average, international undergraduates can anticipate costs ranging from €6,000 to €15,000 annually.

Public universities typically offer more affordable tuition compared to private counterparts. Moreover, EU/EEA students often enjoy lower fees compared to non-EU/EEA peers.

2. Master's Programs:

Master's degree tuition fees for international students tend to be higher than those for bachelor's programs.

The average range falls between €8,000 to €20,000 per annum.

Variations exist depending on the institution's nature, study focus, and EU/EEA residency status.

3. Institutional Diversity:

Higher education in the Netherlands encompasses research universities, universities of applied sciences (HBO), and private entities.

Each institution type may feature distinct fee structures, with research universities typically setting slightly higher rates.

4. Specialized Programs:

Specialized disciplines like medicine, dentistry, and select engineering fields may incur elevated tuition fees due to unique demands like lab equipment and clinical rotations.

Duration of study and program scarcity may further influence pricing.

5. Ancillary Expenses:

Aside from tuition, students must budget for accommodation, health coverage, textbooks, transportation, and personal needs.

A holistic financial plan considers these ancillary costs for a well-rounded budget.

6. Scholarship Availability:

Despite the financial commitment, a plethora of scholarships exist to assist international students in offsetting expenses.

Opportunities span government, institutional, private, and international sectors.

Early scholarship exploration and application enhance the likelihood of securing financial support.

Understanding the nuances of tuition fees for international study in the Netherlands empowers aspirants to make informed choices and navigate the educational landscape with confidence.

Financial Support Options for International Students

Securing funding for higher education can be a daunting task for international students planning to study abroad. Fortunately, the Netherlands provides an extensive range of financial assistance programs, including scholarships, grants, and financial aid. Here's a closer look at these opportunities:

1. Government Scholarships:

The Dutch government offers various scholarship programs to support international students.

One such initiative is the   , designed to aid non-EEA students pursuing bachelor's or master's degrees in the Netherlands. It provides partial tuition coverage for a single academic year.

Additionally, the Orange Knowledge Program offers scholarships to professionals from specific countries for short courses, master's programs, or tailor-made training programs at Dutch institutions.

2. Institutional Scholarships:

Many Dutch universities and colleges provide scholarships tailored specifically to international students.

These scholarships may be awarded based on academic excellence, financial need, chosen field of study, or other criteria.

For example, the University of Amsterdam offers the Amsterdam Merit Scholarship, which covers tuition and living expenses for exceptional non-EEA students enrolling in master's programs.

3. External Scholarships:

External organizations, foundations, and corporations also offer scholarships to international students studying in the Netherlands.

These scholarships may target particular nationalities, academic disciplines, or minority groups.

For instance, the Fulbright Program offers scholarships to U.S. students for graduate study or research in the Netherlands.

4. Erasmus+ Program:

The Erasmus+ Program, an initiative of the European Union, supports international mobility and collaboration in higher education.

Through this program, students may be eligible for scholarships to study abroad in European countries, including the Netherlands.

The Erasmus Mundus Joint Master Degrees offer full scholarships for master's programs across various fields.

5. Research Grants and Fellowships:

Students engaged in research-intensive programs may access grants and fellowships to support their academic pursuits.

These funding opportunities assist with research projects, conference attendance, fieldwork, and other scholarly activities.

Institutions, government agencies, and private foundations commonly provide research funding for students.

6. Institutional Financial Aid:

In addition to scholarships, universities and colleges may offer financial aid such as need-based grants, tuition waivers, or low-interest loans.

International students are encouraged to inquire about available financial aid options at their chosen institutions, ensuring they understand eligibility criteria and application processes.

By exploring and applying for these financial support options, international students can pursue their academic ambitions in the Netherlands with greater ease and confidence.

Living Expenses and Effective Budgeting for Students in the Netherlands

Comprehending the cost of living and adopting efficient budgeting strategies are pivotal for international students preparing to study in the Netherlands. Here's a detailed exploration of living expenses and practical budgeting advice:

1. Living Costs:

Living expenses in the Netherlands fluctuate based on factors like location, lifestyle preferences, and housing choices.

Typically, international students should budget around €800 to €1,200 monthly to cover living expenses.

Key components of living costs include housing, food, transportation, health insurance, educational materials, and personal expenditures.

2. Accommodation:

Accommodation fees represent a substantial portion of the monthly budget. Options range from university dormitories to private rentals. Rental prices vary by city and neighborhood, with larger cities like Amsterdam commanding higher rates.

Sharing accommodation or opting for student housing can help reduce expenses.

3. Food and Groceries:

Buying groceries and cooking at home tend to be more economical than dining out.

Availing oneself of student discounts at supermarkets and local markets can lead to savings.

Strategic meal planning, bulk purchasing, and minimizing food waste contribute to efficient budgeting.

4. Transportation:

Public transportation is a popular choice for getting around in the Netherlands.

Many cities offer discounted transit passes for students, granting access to buses, trams, trains, and metros at reduced fares.

Investing in a bicycle is a cost-effective and environmentally friendly mode of transport.

5. Health Insurance:

Health insurance is mandatory for all residents in the Netherlands, including international students.

Universities often provide discounted health insurance options tailored to student needs.

Selecting a plan that aligns with one's requirements and budget is crucial.

6. Study Materials and Miscellaneous Expenses:

Budgeting for textbooks, course materials, and academic resources is essential.

Utilizing second-hand bookstores, online platforms, and library resources can yield savings.

Allocating funds for occasional expenses such as leisure activities and personal necessities is advisable, while prioritizing essential outlays to prevent overspending.

7. Part-time Employment:

International students are permitted to work part-time while studying in the Netherlands.

Seeking part-time job opportunities, such as tutoring or hospitality roles, can supplement income.

Striking a balance between work commitments and academic duties ensures academic success.

8. Budget Management:

Formulating a monthly budget delineating expected income and expenditures is prudent.

Regularly monitoring expenses and adjusting the budget as necessary fosters financial stability.

Leveraging budgeting tools like apps or spreadsheets aids in tracking spending patterns and identifying areas for economizing.

By grasping the nuances of living costs and employing savvy budgeting tactics, international students can effectively manage their finances and relish a rewarding academic experience in the Netherlands.

Chapter 5: Living in the Netherlands

Living in the Netherlands offers a unique blend of rich cultural experiences, efficient infrastructure, and diverse accommodation options. Let's delve into various aspects of living in the Netherlands, including accommodation choices, transportation methods, and tips for cultural adaptation.

Accommodation Choices in the Netherlands

Securing suitable housing is a pivotal aspect of settling into life as an international student in the Netherlands. The country presents a range of accommodation options tailored to diverse preferences and budgets. Let's delve further into these selections:

- Student Housing:

Dutch universities and educational institutions commonly offer dedicated student housing facilities.

These accommodations encompass dormitories, student residences, or apartments situated either on or near campus grounds.

Student housing aims to foster a sense of community among students and provides convenience regarding access to campus amenities and academic resources.

The array of student housing options varies in terms of amenities, room configurations, and rental rates, with some institutions providing catered and self-catered alternatives.

- Private Rentals:

Many students opt for private rentals, seeking increased independence and privacy.

Private rentals encompass apartments, studios, shared houses, and individual rooms available in the private housing market.

Renting privately affords students greater flexibility concerning location, living arrangements, and lifestyle preferences.

Rental properties differ in size, amenities, and rental costs, influenced by factors such as location, proximity to transportation, and market demand.

- Homestays:

Homestays offer a distinctive avenue for cultural immersion and personal interaction with Dutch families.

In a homestay setup, students reside with a local family in their residence, engaging in shared meals, activities, and daily routines.

Homestays provide a nurturing environment for international students to practice the Dutch language, acquaint themselves with Dutch customs, and gain insights into local culture.

Accommodation in a homestay typically includes a private room, meals, and access to communal household facilities.

- Temporary Accommodation:

Initially, international students may require temporary lodging while they search for more permanent housing.

Temporary accommodation options comprise hostels, short-stay apartments, and temporary housing services offered by universities or housing agencies.

These temporary arrangements afford students a transitional residence while they acclimate to the city, attend orientation programs, and explore long-term housing solutions.

- Online Platforms and Housing Agencies: Online platforms and housing agencies serve as valuable resources for students in their accommodation quest.

Websites like Kamernet, Pararius, and HousingAnywhere facilitate the search for rental properties, enabling students to filter search criteria and communicate directly with landlords.

Housing agencies and student housing organizations may extend assistance in locating accommodation, navigating rental agreements, and addressing housing-related concerns.

Navigating the accommodation landscape in the Netherlands entails thoughtful consideration of factors such as location, budget, lifestyle preferences, and lease terms. Through thorough exploration of the available accommodation options, international students can secure a suitable residence during their tenure in the Netherlands.

Getting around: Public transportation, cycling culture, and exploring Dutch cities

Discovering the Netherlands is made effortless by its efficient public transport system and thriving cycling culture. Moreover, Dutch cities are teeming with attractions awaiting exploration. Let's delve deeper into these facets:

- Public Transport:

The Netherlands boasts a comprehensive and reliable public transport network comprising trains, buses, trams, and metros.

Known for its punctuality and accessibility, Dutch public transport is favored by residents and visitors alike.

Students enjoy discounted travel options like the OV-chipkaart, providing access to all modes of transport at reduced fares.

Public transport facilitates city exploration, campus commutes, and intercity travel within the Netherlands and neighboring regions.

- Cycling Lifestyle:

Cycling is deeply ingrained in Dutch society, evident in its extensive network of bike lanes and bike-friendly infrastructure.

Dutch cities prioritize cycling as a sustainable mode of transport, promoting eco-friendly mobility solutions.

Many students embrace biking as their primary means of getting around, appreciating its health benefits and affordability.

Renting or purchasing a bike is straightforward, with rental shops and second-hand markets abundant in most cities.

- Discovering Dutch Cities:

Dutch cities offer a diverse range of attractions, from historical landmarks to vibrant markets and cultural hubs.

Amsterdam charms with its scenic canals and world-class museums, including the Rijksmuseum and Van Gogh Museum.

Rotterdam captivates with its modern architecture and iconic landmarks like the Markthal and Erasmus Bridge.

Utrecht's medieval charm and iconic Dom Tower create a captivating atmosphere, while The Hague boasts historic sites and cultural institutions.

- Cultural Immersion:

Immersing oneself in Dutch transportation customs and cultural practices is integral to assimilating into Dutch life.

Engaging in cycling events, navigating neighborhoods by bike, and observing traffic regulations aid in acclimatizing to Dutch cycling culture.

Exploring cities on foot, visiting museums, attending cultural events, and interacting with locals deepen one's understanding and appreciation of Dutch culture.

- Sustainability Focus:

The Netherlands prioritizes sustainability and environmental stewardship, reflected in its transport initiatives.

Embracing cycling aligns with Dutch values of eco-consciousness and reducing carbon footprints.

Public transport initiatives, like electric buses and renewable-powered trains, underscore the country's commitment to sustainable mobility.

Navigating Dutch cities and embracing local transport culture offer international students a unique chance to immerse themselves in Dutch life, explore urban landscapes, and connect with communities. By embracing public transport, cycling, and cultural exploration, students can enrich their study abroad experience in the Netherlands.

Adapting to Dutch Culture and Integrating into Society

Transitioning into life in the Netherlands involves immersing oneself in its cultural intricacies and social dynamics. Here are strategies for international students to navigate cultural adaptation and blend seamlessly into Dutch society:

1. Language Proficiency:

While English is widely spoken, learning Dutch enhances cultural assimilation.

Enroll in language courses, practice conversing with locals, and consume Dutch media to hone language skills.

Speaking Dutch not only facilitates communication but also demonstrates respect for the local culture.

2. Embracing Directness:

Dutch communication is known for its candidness and directness.

Embrace transparent communication, express opinions assertively, and appreciate constructive criticism.

Understand that forthrightness is valued and fosters clear understanding in interactions.

3. Cycling Lifestyle:

Cycling is deeply ingrained in Dutch culture, offering a unique way to explore the country.

Embrace biking as a mode of transport, join cycling events, and adhere to traffic rules.

Participating in biking activities fosters a deeper connection with Dutch culture.

4. Social Integration:

Engage in social gatherings, clubs, and events to forge connections with Dutch locals.

Join student organizations, sports clubs, or cultural groups to expand your social network.

Attending festivals and community events provides insights into Dutch traditions and customs.

5. Balancing Work and Leisure:

Dutch society values work-life balance, emphasizing leisure and social activities.

Respect boundaries between work and personal life, prioritize downtime, and embrace Dutch concepts like gezelligheid.

Participating in social gatherings enhances integration into Dutch social circles.

6. Respect and Open-Mindedness:

Approach cultural differences with curiosity and respect.

Honor Dutch customs and traditions, even if they differ from your own, and show interest in local culture.

Being open-minded fosters mutual understanding and acceptance within the community.

7. Utilizing Support Services:

Seek assistance from university resources and support services for guidance on cultural adaptation.

Connect with international student advisors, mentors, or peer support groups for insights and assistance.

Don't hesitate to ask questions or seek help when facing challenges during the adaptation process.

By actively engaging with Dutch culture, building relationships with locals, and embracing new experiences, international students can seamlessly integrate into Dutch society and enrich their study abroad journey in the Netherlands.

Chapter 6: Academic Life and Campus Culture

Embarking on your academic journey in the Netherlands entails delving into a vibrant academic environment characterized by unique classroom dynamics, diverse extracurricular opportunities, and a rich social fabric. Let's explore these facets in detail:

Academic calendar and grading system in the Netherlands

Getting acquainted with the academic calendar and grading system is crucial for navigating academic life in the Netherlands. Here's an in-depth look at these aspects:

1. Academic Calendar:

Dutch universities typically operate on a two-semester system.

The Fall Semester runs from September to January, marking the first half of the academic year.

The Spring Semester spans from February to June, constituting the latter part of the academic year.

Each semester is divided into periods, usually lasting from six to ten weeks.

Courses are structured to align with these periods, varying in duration from single-period to multi-period courses.

2. Grading System:

Grading in Dutch higher education follows a scale from 1 to 10, with 10 representing the highest achievable grade.

Grades are determined by various assessments, such as exams, assignments, presentations, and class participation.

Unlike systems where a score of 5 is a passing grade, in the Netherlands, a grade of 6 or higher is typically required to pass a course.

Grading criteria may differ across courses and disciplines, with some emphasizing theory while others focus on practical application or projects.

Feedback on assessments is commonly provided to aid students in their learning process.

3. Examination Periods:

Examination periods occur at the end of each semester or period, allowing students to sit for final exams or submit major assignments. These periods are scheduled to give students ample time for preparation and completion of assessments.

The duration of examination periods may vary based on university policies and program requirements.

4. Continuous Assessment:

Many courses in the Netherlands employ continuous assessment throughout the semester.

This entails ongoing evaluation of student performance through assignments, quizzes, presentations, and participation.

Continuous assessment fosters student engagement and enables instructors to gauge progress effectively.

5. Academic Integrity and Plagiarism:

Dutch universities uphold rigorous standards of academic integrity, prohibiting plagiarism and other forms of academic misconduct.

Students are expected to adhere to ethical principles in their academic work and familiarize themselves with university policies regarding academic integrity.

Any instances of plagiarism or cheating are dealt with through disciplinary measures.

Understanding the academic calendar and grading system empowers international students to navigate their academic journey in the Netherlands effectively. By grasping these fundamentals, students can plan their studies, manage their workload, and strive for academic excellence.

Classroom dynamics and teaching styles

In Dutch higher education, classroom dynamics and teaching methods emphasize collaboration, interaction, and student engagement. Let's delve deeper into these aspects:

1. Interactive Learning Environment:

Dutch classrooms prioritize active student involvement and encourage open dialogue between students and instructors.

Instead of traditional lectures, classes often involve discussions, group activities, case studies, and problem-solving exercises.

Students are urged to ask questions, voice opinions, and challenge ideas, fostering dynamic exchanges of perspectives.

2. Small Group Discussions and Debates:

Many courses incorporate small group discussions and debates to encourage deeper exploration of course content.

Students work together to analyze concepts, share insights, and enhance critical thinking skills through dialogue and debate.

These discussions provide platforms for students to express thoughts, defend viewpoints, and engage in constructive argumentation.

3. Problem-Based Learning (PBL) and Project-Based Assignments:

Problem-based learning (PBL) is prevalent in Dutch universities, particularly in fields like medicine, law, and engineering.

PBL involves presenting students with real-world problems or case studies, which they collectively analyze, research, and solve.

Project-based assignments are also common, allowing students to apply theoretical knowledge to practical scenarios and develop hands-on skills.

4. Flipped Classroom Model:

The flipped classroom model is increasingly used in Dutch higher education, especially in STEM disciplines.

In this model, students review course material independently before class using online resources.

Classroom time focuses on interactive activities, discussions, and problem-solving, with instructors facilitating learning.

5. Student-Centered Approach:

Dutch teaching styles emphasize student-centered learning, where students actively participate in their education.

Instructors act as facilitators, encouraging self-directed learning, critical inquiry, and independent problem-solving.

Assessment methods include individual and group assignments, presentations, and peer evaluations, reflecting collaborative learning.

6. Practical Application and Real-World Relevance:

Many courses emphasize applying knowledge and skills to real-world situations.

Case studies, simulations, and hands-on exercises provide tangible examples and prepare students for professional contexts.

Guest lectures, industry partnerships, and field trips offer insights into current practices and trends.

In summary, Dutch classrooms prioritize active learning, collaboration, and critical thinking, with teaching methods designed to engage students and deepen their understanding of course material. By actively participating in discussions and activities, students can maximize their learning experience and develop essential skills for success.

Extracurricular activities, student organizations, and social life on campus

In the Netherlands, university life extends beyond academics, offering a diverse array of extracurricular pursuits, student-led organizations, and vibrant social engagements. Here's a closer look at the myriad of opportunities available:

- Extracurricular Pursuits:

Dutch universities host a broad spectrum of extracurricular activities catering to varied interests.

These include sports clubs, cultural societies, artistic groups, academic associations, volunteer initiatives, and more.

Students can partake in sports tournaments, music ensembles, theater productions, language exchanges, and community projects. Engaging in extracurriculars enables students to explore interests, cultivate skills, and connect beyond academic realms.

- Student Organizations:

Dutch campuses thrive with student-led groups and associations covering diverse areas.

These encompass academic interests, cultural diversity, hobbies, and social causes.

Students can join clubs aligned with their studies, engage in student governance, or advocate for causes like sustainability or social justice.

These groups foster leadership, networking, and enriching campus and community contributions.

- Campus Social Life:

Campus life buzzes with social activities, ranging from events to themed nights and festivals.

Students gather at campus spots like cafes, lounges, and student hubs for socializing, studying, and unwinding.

Event listings on social media and university platforms facilitate student communication and coordination.

- Integration Initiatives for International Students:

Universities often provide tailored integration activities for international students.

These encompass orientations, buddy systems, cultural outings, fostering adjustment to Dutch culture and campus life. Such initiatives encourage intercultural connections and mutual learning among international and local peers.

- Community Engagement Opportunities: Students can also engage with the local community through volunteering, internships, and outreach endeavors. University partnerships with local entities offer avenues for community involvement and service learning.

Active participation fosters practical experience, meaningful contributions, and broadened perspectives beyond campus confines.

In summary, campus extracurriculars, student organizations, and social gatherings play pivotal roles in enhancing the university experience in the Netherlands. By embracing these opportunities, students can enrich their academic journey, forge lasting bonds, and foster a sense of belonging within the university community.

Chapter 7: Language and Cultural Challenges

Embarking on a study journey in the Netherlands entails encountering language and cultural nuances that may present challenges for international students.

Language barriers and resources for learning Dutch

Encountering language hurdles is a common experience for international students in the Netherlands, where Dutch serves as the primary language. Below is an extensive look at language barriers and the available Dutch learning aids:

- Language Hurdles:

International students often confront language obstacles in social, academic, and administrative spheres.

Despite widespread English proficiency, certain interactions, especially with older demographics or in rural locales, necessitate Dutch proficiency.

Grasping Dutch language and culture enhances integration, fosters communication, and enriches the study abroad journey.

- Dutch Learning Resources:

Dutch Language Courses: Many Dutch universities offer tailored Dutch language programs catering to international students. These courses span various proficiency levels and encompass speaking, listening, reading, and writing skills.

Language Schools: Across the Netherlands, numerous language institutions provide intensive Dutch language courses, accommodating international student needs with flexible schedules and intimate class settings.

Online Learning Platforms: Abundant online resources like Duolingo, Babbel, and Rosetta Stone furnish interactive Dutch learning modules, accommodating self-paced learning through exercises and tutorials.

Language Exchange Initiatives: Engaging in language exchange programs pairs international students with Dutch-speaking counterparts keen on learning the students' native tongue. This reciprocal setup fosters language practice and cultural exchange in a supportive milieu.

Language Cafes and Groups: Many Dutch cities host language cafes and conversational meet-ups, offering relaxed environments for practicing Dutch. These gatherings afford opportunities to interact with native speakers and refine language skills through real-world dialogue.

- Immersive Experiences:

Embedding oneself in Dutch language and culture proves highly efficacious for language acquisition. Living with Dutch peers, partaking in local activities, and attending cultural events provide immersive contexts conducive to language learning.

Actively seeking chances to employ Dutch in daily scenarios—such as shopping, dining out, or using public transport—bolsters confidence and fluency.

- . University Support Services:

Universities extend support services for international students endeavoring to learn Dutch, offering language advisors, labs, and conversation circles.

International student groups may organize language exchanges, study circles, or cultural outings to facilitate language acquisition and cultural assimilation.

By leveraging these resources and actively participating in language learning endeavors, international students can surmount language barriers, refine their communication aptitude, and fully immerse themselves in Dutch culture during their Dutch study abroad stint.

Understanding Dutch customs, etiquette, and cultural norms

Gaining insight into Dutch customs, etiquette, and cultural standards is essential for international students navigating interactions and blending into Dutch society seamlessly. Here's a comprehensive look:

- Direct Communication:

Dutch communication emphasizes honesty and directness, valuing clear expression of opinions and engaging in open debates without reservation.

- Punctuality:

Timeliness holds high regard, with arriving promptly to appointments, meetings, and social gatherings considered a sign of respect and reliability.

- Informality and Equality:

Dutch society embraces informality and equality, evident in addressing individuals by their first names regardless of age or status, fostering open dialogue and diminishing hierarchical barriers.

- Personal Space:

Respecting personal space is key, with Dutch people valuing a comfortable distance during interactions, and encroaching on others' space perceived as intrusive.

- Tolerance and Diversity:

The Netherlands prides itself on its inclusive attitudes, welcoming diversity in ethnicity, religion, sexual orientation, and lifestyle choices, with discrimination not tolerated.

- Environmental Awareness:

Sustainability ranks high on the Dutch agenda, with recycling, cycling, and public transportation widely practiced to reduce environmental impact.

- Cycling Culture:

Renowned for its cycling culture, the Netherlands advocates understanding cycling rules and etiquette to navigate roads and paths safely, demonstrating respect for this integral aspect of Dutch life.

By acquainting themselves with these cultural nuances, international students can integrate smoothly into Dutch society, fostering positive relationships and embracing the Dutch way of life.

Overcoming cultural differences and building cross-cultural competence

Successfully traversing cultural gaps and enhancing cross-cultural proficiency proves pivotal for international students adjusting to life in the Netherlands. Here's a more nuanced exploration:

1. Awareness and Openness:

Acknowledging and embracing cultural disparities with an open attitude marks the initial stride towards bolstering cross-cultural proficiency.

Recognizing that cultural norms and values may diverge from one's own background fosters understanding and acceptance.

2. Active Listening and Observation:

Actively tuning into others' perspectives and observing cultural subtleties in social interactions heightens cultural acumen.

Noting non-verbal cues, gestures, and expressions furnishes invaluable insights into cultural dynamics.

3. Cultural Sensitivity and Respect:

Exhibiting sensitivity and respect towards cultural distinctions lies at the core of honing cross-cultural competence.

Eschewing stereotypes, refraining from preemptive judgments, and valuing diverse viewpoints underpin positive intercultural rapport.

4. Adaptability and Flexibility:

Nurturing adaptability and flexibility equips individuals to navigate unfamiliar cultural terrains adeptly.

Embracing novel experiences, adjusting communication styles, and embracing varied customs contribute to seamless cross-cultural interactions.

5. Effective Communication Strategies:

Crafting effective communication strategies tailored to diverse cultural milieus fosters mutual understanding and minimizes misinterpretations.

Deploying active listening, elucidating messages, and soliciting feedback nurture lucid and respectful communication across cultural divides.

6. Cultural Immersion and Engagement:

Immersement in cultural encounters, be it partaking in local festivities, volunteering within the community, or engaging in cultural exchange programs, enriches comprehension and appreciation of diverse cultures.

Interacting with natives, absorbing their customs, traditions, and values firsthand, augments cross-cultural learning and forges meaningful bonds.

7. Reflective Practice and Ongoing Learning:

Engaging in reflective contemplation encourages individuals to scrutinize their own cultural predispositions, assumptions, and conducts.

Embracing a perpetually inquisitive stance and an ethos of perpetual growth empowers individuals to refine their cross-cultural adeptness over time.

By actively embracing these strategies, international students can bridge cultural divergences, refine cross-cultural proficiency, and flourish within diverse multicultural milieus, both within the Netherlands and beyond.

Chapter 8: Employment and Career Opportunities

Navigating employment and career prospects is a crucial aspect of the study experience in the Netherlands for international students. Here's an in-depth exploration of key points:

Regulations for International Students' Work Permits

Understanding the intricacies of work permit regulations is vital for international students aiming to secure employment while studying in the Netherlands. Here's a thorough breakdown:

- Conditions of Residence Permits: International students from non-EU/EEA nations typically require a residence permit (student visa) to study in the Netherlands. Work permits for international students often hinge on their residence permits, subject to specific conditions.
- Part-Time Employment During Studies: Students with valid residence permits are allowed to engage in part-time work during their academic pursuits in the Netherlands. Part-time employment usually has a weekly hour limit, typically ranging from 10 to 20

hours, contingent on seasonal factors and job type.

- Prerequisites for Work Permits:

Non-EU/EEA students may need a separate work permit, aside from their residence permits, for employment in the Netherlands. Work permit issuance is contingent on various criteria, encompassing job nature, duration, and employer adherence to labor regulations.

- Exemptions and Special Cases:

Certain student categories might be exempt from the need for a separate work permit.

For instance, students enrolled in accredited programs at Dutch research universities or universities of applied sciences could qualify for exemption, permitting work sans a separate permit.

- Summer and Full-Time Work Opportunities:

International students may be allowed to work full-time during official holiday periods, like summer breaks, without surpassing the usual hourly limit.

Adhering to specific regulations and conditions for summer and full-time employment is crucial to ensure compliance.

- Employer Responsibilities:

Employers hiring international students must adhere to Dutch labor laws, encompassing minimum wage standards, working conditions, and employee rights. Compliance may necessitate notifying relevant authorities and furnishing documentation verifying the student's work eligibility in the Netherlands.

- Renewal and Prolongation:

Work permits for international students typically align with the duration of their study programs and might necessitate renewal or extension in case of program changes or prolonged stays.

Familiarizing oneself with work permit regulations is pivotal for international students to comply with Dutch immigration and labor statutes while seeking employment opportunities during their tenure in the Netherlands. Seeking guidance from university international offices or immigration authorities can offer clarity on specific requisites and processes for obtaining work permits.

Internship opportunities and gaining practical experience during your studies

Delving into internship opportunities and gaining hands-on experience is invaluable for international students during their studies in the Netherlands. Here's an expanded discussion:

- Diverse Internship Landscape:

The Netherlands offers a dynamic array of internship opportunities across various industries, providing international students with abundant chances to gain practical experience.

Sectors like technology, finance, engineering, marketing, and hospitality actively recruit interns, offering exposure to real-world scenarios and industry practices.

- University Support and Resources:

Many Dutch universities feature dedicated career centers or internship offices, aiding students in securing internships aligned with their academic and career goals.

These services offer assistance with resume crafting, interview readiness, and networking tactics to bolster students' internship prospects.

- Academic Integration and Credit:

Internships are often integrated into academic programs, enabling students to earn credits while acquiring hands-on experience. Some universities mandate internships as part of their curriculum, providing avenues for applying theoretical knowledge in practical settings and honing transferable skills.

- Networking and Industry Ties:

Internships serve as invaluable networking platforms, enabling students to forge connections with professionals in their field, expand their industry contacts, and broaden their professional circle.

Cultivating meaningful relationships with supervisors, peers, and industry mentors during internships can pave the way for future job opportunities and career growth.

- Skill Development and Career Readiness:

Internships offer opportunities for students to cultivate essential skills such as teamwork, communication, problem-solving, and project management.

Hands-on experience in professional environments enhances students' employability and readies them for the transition from academia to the workforce.

- International Internship Programs:

Numerous companies in the Netherlands extend international internship programs tailored to international students, fostering cultural exchange and global collaboration. Participating in such initiatives enables students to gain cross-cultural exposure, broaden their perspectives, and develop intercultural competencies.

- Post-Internship Prospects:

Internships often serve as springboards to future career opportunities, with many firms extending full-time employment offers to exceptional interns post-graduation.

Demonstrating commendable performance, exhibiting initiative, and fostering a positive reputation during internships heightens students' chances of securing employment offers upon graduation.

By actively pursuing internship opportunities, international students can enrich their academic journey, acquire practical proficiencies, expand their professional network, and bolster their employability in the competitive job market.

Post-graduation options: Job search strategies, entrepreneurship, and staying in the Netherlands after graduation

Upon completing their studies in the Netherlands, international students have a range of paths to consider, including job search tactics, entrepreneurial pursuits, and options for remaining in the country. Here's an in-depth look:

1. Job Search Tactics:

International graduates can utilize diverse strategies to secure employment in the Netherlands, such as online job portals, networking via platforms like LinkedIn, attending career events, and tapping into university alumni networks.

Crafting tailored resumes and cover letters, emphasizing relevant experiences, and preparing for interviews in English or Dutch are pivotal elements of the job hunt.

2. Entrepreneurship:

The Netherlands harbors a vibrant startup environment, appealing to budding entrepreneurs.

Graduates with innovative business concepts can explore entrepreneurial avenues through startup incubators, accelerators, and shared workspaces.

Government initiatives like the Dutch Startup Visa program facilitate entrepreneurship for non-EU/EEA nationals, offering pathways to establish and expand businesses in the Netherlands.

3. Remaining in the Netherlands:

International graduates have the option to stay in the Netherlands post-graduation for job prospects or further studies.

The Orientation Year (zoekjaar) visa enables recent Dutch university alumni to reside in the country for up to a year while seeking employment.

Upon securing qualifying job offers, graduates can apply for residence permits under schemes like the highly skilled migrant program or other relevant visa categories to continue living and working in the Netherlands.

4. Permanent Residency and Citizenship:

Graduates aspiring for long-term settlement in the Netherlands can pursue permanent residency or Dutch citizenship over time. Permanent residency typically requires five years of continuous legal residence, fulfilling income criteria, and passing integration exams.

Dutch citizenship can be attained through naturalization after meeting residency duration, language proficiency, and civic integration requisites.

5. Career Support Services:

Universities and career centers extend continuous aid to international graduates in their career pursuits.

Services like career counseling, job search workshops, resume refinement, and mock interviews equip graduates with tools to navigate the job market and advance professionally within the Netherlands.

By exploring these post-graduation avenues and leveraging available support, international students can smoothly transition into the workforce, embark on entrepreneurial ventures, and forge rewarding careers in the Netherlands.

Chapter 9: Health and Well-being

Maintaining good health and well-being is essential for international students studying in the Netherlands. Let's delve into the healthcare system, health insurance requirements, mental health support services, and strategies for maintaining a healthy work-life balance.

Healthcare System in the Netherlands and Health Insurance Obligations for Students

The Netherlands boasts a comprehensive healthcare system renowned for its accessibility and quality of care, which is crucial for international students studying in the country. Here's a simplified overview:

1. Universal Coverage:

The Dutch healthcare system operates on the principle of universal coverage, ensuring that all residents, including international students, have access to essential medical services through a mix of public and private providers.

2. Public Health Insurance (Basisverzekering):

Public health insurance, known as basisverzekering, covers fundamental medical needs like visits to general practitioners, hospital stays, prescription medications, and maternity care.

International students under 30 working less than 56 hours monthly usually qualify for this public insurance.

3. Private Health Insurance (Aanvullende Verzekering):

Besides public insurance, students may opt for private insurance (aanvullende verzekering) for additional coverage, like dental care, physiotherapy, or mental health services.

While public insurance is compulsory for basic needs, private insurance offers supplementary benefits, though it's optional.

4. Insurance Mandates for Students:

It's a legal requirement for international students in the Netherlands to hold health insurance.

Within four months of registering their Dutch address, students must obtain health coverage to avoid penalties.

5. Access to Services:

Once insured, students gain access to a wide array of healthcare providers, including GPs, specialists, hospitals, and pharmacies, known for their excellence and patient-centered care. Booking appointments with GPs for non-emergency issues and seeking specialized care through referrals or directly are standard procedures.

Understanding the Dutch healthcare system, adhering to insurance obligations, and choosing appropriate coverage options guarantee that international students have access to quality healthcare, allowing them to focus on their studies with peace of mind.

Enhancing Mental Health Support Services and Resources

Prioritizing mental health assistance is crucial for international students in the Netherlands. Here's a deeper look at the available support services and resources:

1. University Counseling Services:

Dutch universities offer customized counseling services to address students' mental health needs.

Trained counselors deliver confidential support for stress, anxiety, depression, homesickness, academic pressure, and relationship issues.

Services include individual and group therapy sessions, workshops, and educational programs to boost coping skills and resilience.

2. Community Mental Health Centers:

Besides campus services, students can access mental health centers and clinics across the Netherlands.

These centers provide counseling, therapy, psychiatric assessments, and crisis intervention.

Referrals can be made through university counseling centers or directly for ongoing support or specialized treatment.

3. Helplines and Online Resources:

Helplines staffed by trained volunteers or professionals offer 24/7 support and crisis intervention.

Online resources like self-help guides, mental health assessments, and virtual support communities provide accessible help.

Teletherapy platforms and mobile apps offer remote therapy options for students facing barriers to in-person care.

4. Peer Support Groups and Student Organizations:

Peer support groups, led by universities or students, provide safe spaces for sharing experiences and offering mutual support.

Student organizations focused on mental health awareness raise awareness and promote mental health literacy through events and workshops.

5. Cultural and Multilingual Support:

Culturally sensitive and multilingual mental health services cater to international students' unique needs.

Some universities offer counseling in multiple languages or provide interpreters for effective communication.

Culturally competent professionals ensure effective support aligned with students' cultural backgrounds.

6. Self-Care and Coping Strategies:

Encouraging mindfulness, relaxation, exercise, healthy eating, and sufficient sleep fosters mental well-being.

Incorporating self-care into daily routines and seeking social connections nurture mental health.

Developing coping mechanisms and seeking support when needed are vital aspects of self-care.

By utilizing these mental health services and resources, international students can actively manage their well-being, access timely support, and navigate their study abroad experience with resilience.

Maintaining a Balanced Lifestyle during Studies

Balancing academics with personal well-being is vital for international students in the Netherlands. Here are further tips to achieve this equilibrium:

1. Prioritize Self-Care:

Allocate time for activities like exercise, meditation, hobbies, and relaxation to nurture physical and mental health.

Take regular breaks to prevent burnout and maintain productivity.

2. Establish Boundaries:

Set clear boundaries between study, work, and personal time to safeguard leisure activities.

Learn to decline excessive commitments and prioritize tasks wisely.

3. Effective Time Management:

Utilize tools like planners and digital apps to organize tasks, deadlines, and study sessions effectively.

Break down tasks into manageable segments and set achievable goals.

4. Practice Mindfulness:

Incorporate mindfulness into daily routines through mindful breathing, walking, or eating to reduce stress and foster awareness.

5. Cultivate Social Connections:

Forge meaningful relationships with peers, professors, and locals to combat loneliness.

Engage in social activities and join clubs or organizations to build a support network.

6. Realistic Expectations:

Set realistic academic goals and acknowledge that perfection is unattainable.

Focus on progress and celebrate accomplishments, regardless of size.

7. Leisure Planning:

Schedule leisure activities such as city exploration, hobbies, or social gatherings to rejuvenate.

Integrate leisure into weekly schedules for a balanced lifestyle.

8. Seek Support:

Reach out to university services, advisors, or trusted individuals for assistance when feeling overwhelmed.

Remember that seeking help is a strength and support is available when needed.

By implementing these strategies, international students can cultivate a harmonious work-life balance, enhancing their well-being and academic success in the Netherlands.

Chapter 10: Conclusion and Next Steps

As you come to the end of your study journey in the Netherlands, take a moment to reflect on your experiences, keep in touch with your international contacts, and explore additional resources for support and information. Here's a detailed look:

1. Reflecting on Your Study Abroad Experience:

Pause to ponder on the academic, personal, and cultural aspects of your time in the Netherlands.

Consider the challenges you faced, the lessons learned, and the personal growth achieved during your study abroad venture.

Recall the friendships forged, cultural insights gained, and cherished memories made along the way.

2. Tips for Staying Connected and Utilizing Your International Network:

Stay in contact with friends, peers, professors, and other connections from your time in the Netherlands.

Use various communication platforms to maintain meaningful relationships and tap into your international network for career prospects, cultural exchange, and personal development.

Explore opportunities to join alumni groups, professional networks, or online communities to continue fostering connections with fellow expats.

3. Resources for Further Information and Assistance:

Explore the support services offered by your university, including alumni assistance, career guidance, and international student support.

Stay updated on educational, career, and cultural opportunities through online platforms, newsletters, and alumni channels.

Research organizations, governmental bodies, and online forums providing resources and aid for international students transitioning back home or planning further global adventures.

Engage in mentorship programs, webinars, and workshops to further your personal and academic growth post-study abroad.

As you move forward, remember to cherish your experiences, maintain connections with your international network, and continue seeking opportunities for learning and development. Your time in the Netherlands has equipped you with valuable skills, perspectives, and connections that will enrich

your future endeavors.

Appendices

Glossary of Dutch Terms Related to Education and Student Life:

Understanding Dutch terminology related to education and student life is essential for international students studying in the Netherlands. Here's an expanded glossary to aid in navigating the academic landscape:

- Hogeschool: Refers to a University of Applied Sciences, offering practical-oriented education in fields such as engineering, business, and applied arts.

- Universiteit: Denotes a research university, focusing on theoretical and academic study across various disciplines.
- Propedeuse: The first-year diploma obtained at universities and universities of applied sciences, usually after completing a specific set of courses.
- Bachelordiploma: The bachelor's degree awarded upon completing a three-year undergraduate program at a university or university of applied sciences.

- Masteropleiding: Refers to a master's program, typically lasting one or two years, pursued after obtaining a bachelor's degree.
- Collegegeld: Tuition fees charged by educational institutions for attending courses and programs.
- Studiefinanciering: Student finance provided by the Dutch government, including loans, grants, and travel discounts.
- OV-kaart: Public transportation card available to eligible students, providing

discounted or free travel on buses, trams, and trains.

- Studievereniging: Student association associated with a specific study program or faculty, organizing academic events, social activities, and study-related excursions.
- Studentenvereniging: Student association offering a wide range of social activities, including parties, sports events, and cultural outings.
- Kamernet: Online platform facilitating the search for accommodation,

including shared apartments, student rooms, and studio flats.

- DUO: Dienst Uitvoering Onderwijs, the governmental agency responsible for student finance, educational support, and student loan administration.

- Nuffic: Dutch organization promoting internationalization in education, offering information, resources, and support services for international students.

Directory of Useful Websites, Organizations, and Contact Information

Accessing relevant websites and organizations is crucial for international students to obtain essential information and support during their stay in the Netherlands. Here's are directories to facilitate their search:

- Study in Holland: The official website offering comprehensive information on studying in the Netherlands, including details on programs, scholarships, admission requirements, and practical matters such as visa procedures and housing options. (Website: studyinholland.nl)

- Nuffic: A Dutch organization dedicated to promoting internationalization in education, providing valuable resources, guidance, and support services for international students, including information on scholarships, accreditation, and academic recognition. (Website: nuffic.nl)
- DUO: Dienst Uitvoering Onderwijs is the governmental agency responsible for managing student finance, educational support, and student loan

administration in the Netherlands. International students can find information on student grants, loans, and tuition fees on their website. (Website: duo.nl)

- IND: The Immigration and Naturalization Service provides information and assistance regarding visa and residence permit applications for international students planning to study in the Netherlands. Their website offers guidance on visa requirements, application procedures, and residence permits. (Website: ind.nl)

- Kamernet: An online platform widely used by students to search for accommodation in the Netherlands. Students can browse listings for shared apartments, student rooms, and studio flats in various cities and regions. (Website: kamernet.nl)

- Local Municipality Websites: Each municipality in the Netherlands has its own website, providing information on local services, residence registration, healthcare facilities, and cultural events. Students can find contact details and relevant information for their local municipality online.

- Emergency Contact Numbers: It's essential for international students to be aware of emergency contact numbers for police, ambulance, and fire services in the Netherlands. These numbers vary depending on the region but are typically easy to find online or in local directories.

By utilizing this expanded directory of useful websites, organizations, and contact information, international students can access valuable resources, guidance, and support to enhance their study abroad experience in the Netherlands.

Printed in Great Britain
by Amazon